Taking the Mystery Out of the Menu

Naomi Powell

Clink Street

London | New York

Published by Clink Street Publishing 2017

Copyright © 2017

First edition.

ISBN: 978-1-911110-67-5
E-Book: 978-1-911110-68-2

Acknowledgements

To my amazing husband and best friend, Maurice, for his hours of generous help and endless patience, which enabled me to complete this book. Thank you.

And to my lovely daughter, Corinne, for her helpful advice, encouragement and constant enthusiasm right from the start.

A pocket guide to cuisine and understanding the menu

Introduction

Eating out is not only a 'special event' activity enjoyed by families and friends in our modern high speed world, but very often a necessity for the great work force whose long working day and often unsociable working hours allow little time for home food preparation. However, when eating out for whatever reason, it can be very confusing when presented with a menu of unfamiliar terms and dishes. Often the waiting staff have limited knowledge of what exactly is being cooked-up and served when they take the order, as many are inexperienced or part-time staff, and they too are unfamiliar with new and sophisticated culinary terms and menu inclusions.

'Taking the Mystery out of the Menu' was initially intended to do just that – to shed light on some of the cultural, niche and often ambiguous terms which occur on modern menus in hotels, restaurants and food bars. So, what began as a personal enquiry into the intrigues of modern cuisine terminology, quickly developed from a 'list of the unfamiliar' to what I hope, is now a useful reference text for all enthusiasts of the culinary arts – but also for those who are thinking about making the hotel and catering business their chosen career.

I quickly realised that once I had started compiling the list of unfamiliar terms, that I couldn't just stop at the obviously unusual and cultural references; since I became more and more aware of new and niche 'menu inclusions' – serious research became necessary. As the list lengthened, my book expanded and I found myself with a dictionary of largely unfamiliar though

1

useful terms, which even as a housewife and cook, ruling my own kitchen for many years, I had not previously come across or had failed to memorise or research various terms, even when they had jumped out at me from the pages of recipe books

For those of you who are just happy to enjoy the ambience of restaurants amongst good companions, I hope this little reference guide will tell you something about the flavours and cooking techniques which make up the national and multicultural food identity of these Islands. I also hope it may help you to better understand what you are ordering and to enjoy with confidence the meal which is ultimately served.

A

A

Abalone	Common name of edible sea snails.
Abat, Les	See Offal.
Abattis	Giblets
Abernethy biscuit	Plain sweet biscuit flavoured with caraway.
Affogato (It. Drowned)	Is a coffee based beverage usually with scoop of ice cream with espresso – sometimes with amaretto.
Agave Syrup	A commercially produced sweetener extracted from the Mexican Agave plant. Agave is also used in the production of Tequila. Agave Syrup is available in most supermarkets and Health Food shops.
Aiginatter, Aiginates	Carbohydrates derived from seaweed.
Aigrettes	Cheese savouries.
Aiguillette	A thin strip or slice of cooked poultry, meat or fish.
Aillade	Name given to various sauces, accompaniments for salads, all strongly flavoured with garlic.
Aioli	Garlic flavoured mayonnaise.
À l'Anglaise (English style)	Plainly cooked, usually boiled in stock or water.
À l' Oignon	With onion.

À la Carte	Food prepared or served to order and not part of a set (table d' hôte) meal.
À la Chantilly	Including or accompanied by vanilla flavoured, sweetened whipped cream.
À la Chasseur	Hunters' style, cooked with wine and shallots and garnished with mushrooms.
À la Diable	Highly spiced or devilled.
À la Dubarry	Recipe involving cauliflower.
À la Duchesse	Rich creamed potato served in fancy shapes, or used as topping
Al dente (To the bite)	The cooked texture of food.
Al fresco	Eating out of doors, casual.
Allumettes	Potatoes cut into 'match-sticks' and fried. Sometimes called straw potatoes. Can also be used to describe sweet or pastry fingers.
Almondine, Amondine	Indicates a garnish of almonds.
Aloo bokhara	Dried plums.
Alpestra	Hard dry cheese from the French Alps.
Anardana	Dried and ground pomegranate seeds.
Anchoiade, Anchaiade	A savoury pulp of anchovy and olive base, with herbs, onions, garlic and tomatoes; used as a topping on croutons, toast, etc.
Angelica	Crystalised stem of a herb used as cake decorations.
Anna, Pommes	A classic French potato dish consisting of overlapping slices of potatoes in butter and baked.
Anti-Pasta, Pasto	A dish served before the main course in Italy.
Aperitif	French name for a fairly mild drink taken before meals.
Apple Strudel	Sheets of filo pastry spread with a rich mixture of apple, sultanas, cinnamon, almonds etc. rolled-up to encase filling, and baked.

Appetiser	Starters, finger food served at the beginning of a meal to stimulate the appetite.
Arancini	Mushrooms.
Arbroath Smokies	Whole young haddock or whiting that have been gutted and beheaded, then smoked to a dark bronze colour: Eaten hot and always sold in pairs.
Arctic Flat Bread	A vegetarian flat bread made from wheat and rye flour, yeast and herbs plus agave syrup.
Armagnac	High quality French Brandy.
Arrosoto	Italian baked risotto.
Arrowroot	An edible starch; an excellent thickener and it makes a clear glaze.
Asafoetida	A spice used in Indian cuisine. Can also be used as a condiment
Aspic	Seasoned, flavoured jelly.
Au blanc	White, or white sauce.
Aubergine or Egg Plant	Quite a versatile vegetable though better suited for use in main separate courses rather than as an accompanying vegetable.
Au gratin	A baked dish with a cheese and bread crumb topping.
Au jus	Served with natural juices or gravy.
Avgolemono	A Mediterranean sauce.

NOTES

B

B

Baba	A rich light textured yeast based cake.
Baba Ganouch, Baba Ghanoush	(Arabic) 'Pampered Daddy'. Lebanese dish of cooked egg plant, olive oil seasoning and tahini.
Baguete, Baguette	A long thin loaf of French bread.
Baklava	A Middle Eastern sweet concoction of layers of filo pastry soaked in honey or syrup encasing nuts and spices.
Bain Marie	(Water Bath) A cooking vessel to gently heat food and/or keep it warm over a period of time.
Balcan Stuffing	A stuffing for turkey consisting of onions, rice, currants, heart and liver of turkey, blanched chopped almonds, butter stock, tomato paste and herbs.
Balsamic Vinegar	An Italian vinegar produced from a reduction of white wine/fermented grape juice.
Bannock	A large round oatmeal and barleymeal scone.
Bara brith	A Welsh speckled bread.
Barbue	See under 'Brill'.

Barding	Laying of slices of fat or bacon on breast of a bird before roasting to prevent the flesh from drying out.
Barecole (Kale)	Curley leaved vegetable of cabbage family.
Barm	Brewers' yeast.
Barm Brack	An Irish yeasted fruit bread. Traditionally eaten at Hallowe'en.
Barquette	Small boat-shaped pastry cases for sweet or savoury fillings.
Basting	To spoon hot fat or liquid over meat and poultry at intervals during roasting or baking to prevent the meat drying out and to add flavour.
Bath Olivers	Crisp crackers. Excellent with cheese.
Bavaroise, bavarois	(Bavarian Cream). A dessert similar to pastry cream, thickened with gelatine or isinglass and flavoured with a liqueur. Can also be a hot drink.
Béarnaise	An egg based sauce made with white wine, herbs and butter.
Béchamel	A white sauce with bay leaf, onions and peppercorns added before bringing to the boil.
Beef Dolmades	Stuffed cabbage leaves usually using minced beef.
Beef Flank	(Course flesh), for stews, braising or pot roast.
Beef Pastrimi	Brined meat which is then seasoned, smoked and steamed.
Bhindi	Okra in chickpea-batter
Bien cuit	Well cooked, well done.
Bigos	Polish national dish: Hunters' stew.
Biltong, Bilton	South African flavoured dried beef, similar to 'jerky'.
Binding	To add egg, fat or other liquids to a mixture to 'bind' or hold it together.

Biryani	Traditional Indian rice dish.
Bisque, Bisk	A thick rich fish soup, usually made from white fish stock.
Blanching	To subject food to boiling water in order to whiten it, or to preserve its natural colour, or to loosen skin (as with tomatoes), or to remove a flavour which is too strong.
Blending	The art of mixing dry ingredients with liquid and producing a smooth paste without lumps. Also, mixing different liquids to produce an improved blend.
Blini	Buckwheat pancakes.
Blondies	White chocolate brownies
Bomba or Calasparra Rice	A Spanish variety of rice from Valencia used for Paella.
Bombay Duck	A fish found in Indian Waters, which when dried is often served in curry.
Bortsch	Beetroot soup.
Bottomless	Guests can have more without paying extra.
Boudin	Varieties of sausage with Eastern European, Germanic and American connections.
Bouillabaisse	Fish stew.
Bouillion	A clear soup, usually made from beef.
Bouquet Garni	A small bunch of herbs used to flavour soups and stews.
Bourride	Poached fish fillets in a stock and served on fried bread.
Boxty Bread	A traditional potato bread from Northern Ireland. Sometimes called 'Dippity'.
Bran	A cereal derived from outer layers of grain.
Brill or Barbue	A salt water fish.
Brining	To immerse food in salt water solution.
Brioche	Fancy sweet bread or yeast cake.

Brisling	Sprats, used like sardines.
Brochettes	Skewered meat and vegetables for grilling or barbeque.
Browning	Giving a usually already cooked dish an appetising golden brown finish by placing it beneath a hot grill or into a hot oven, for a short while before serving.
Bruschetta	An Italian starter of grilled bread with garlic dressing, olive oil and salt to which may be added tomatoes, beans other vegetables and cheese or ham.
Brûléed	To burn a sugar topping with a blowtorch or grill, to form a glassy golden brown finish.
Brunaise	A mixture of dried or shredded vegetables used as a base for soup, or as a garnish.
Buckwheat, Saracen Corn	A pseudo-cereal not related to wheat.
Bulgur Wheat	Whole wheat grain, partially pre-cooked; used in Middle Eastern cuisine.
Burrata	A semi soft Italian cheese made from mozzarella and cream surrounded by an outer layer of mozzarella cheese.
Buta misoyaki	Grilled pork shoulder or chops flavoured with ginger, chives, white miso and sesame seeds.
Butterflied	See 'Spatchcocked'.

NOTES

NOTES

C

C

Caesar Salad	An Italian dish incorporating lettuce, bacon, anchovies and croutons.
Canoroli Rice	Risotto rice.
Cannelloni	Meat filled pancakes, covered with two sauces: tomato and white sauce, and topped with grated cheese.
Capons	Neutered cock birds, especially bred to produce good meaty roasts.
Capsicums	Pepper of all varieties.
Caraque	Melted chocolate. Flakes or scrolls of chocolate, cut or shaved from melted chocolate.
Carbonade	(Of beef). Essentially a beef casserole topped with French bread spread with French mustard.
Cardoons	Resemble a giant celery and may be used similarly.
Carolo nero	A green/black member of the cabbage family, which also has a sweet flavour. Used extensively in Italy.
Carpacci	An appetiser comprising ground or thinly sliced or pounded raw meat or fish.
Carrageen	Edible seaweed. Also known as Irish Moss.

Cassata	An elaborate dessert from Sicily incorporating sponge cake, fruit juice or liqueur, ricotta cheese and fruit.
Cassoulet	Originally a French peasant dish. A rich slowly cooked casserole containing meat, typically pork sausages, goose, duck or mutton.
Cawl	A broth. A staple dish of Wales using 'cut-offs' of lamb, bacon and vegetables.
Celeriac	A variety of celery, with the root only used as a vegetable.
Ceriche, Ceviche	A Latin American dish made from raw fish marinated in citrus fruit.
Cevapcici	Yugoslav kebabs.
Chachonka, Shakshouka	A Middle Eastern dish of poached eggs and vegetables in a tomato sauce.
Chacoli	See 'Txakoli'.
Chantenay	See 'Crécy, à la'.
Charlotte Royale	Swiss Roll Cake, A classic dessert incorporating a fruit bavarois.
Chartreuse	A moulded fruit jelly sweet served with cream.
Char	Fresh water fish with oily flesh.
Chard	Green leaves cooked as spinach. Mid stalks cooked as celery.
Chaud froid	(Hot Cold). A sauce used to accompany cooked fish, meat or poultry when served cold as entrees. Or as a sweet sauce made from equal quantities of lemon jelly and cream.
Chawan Mushi	Japanese steamed custard.
Chayote, Mirliton or Mirleton.	A squash type pear shaped vegetable.
Cheese Croutes	Pieces of cheese flavoured toasted bread.
Chermoula	A North African herb.
Chia seeds	Highly nutritious seeds from Mexico.

Chicken Chasseur	A sophisticated Chicken Casserole, incorporating bacon, mushrooms, tomatoes and herbs.
Chickory, Chicory	A herb from which coffee substitute can be made.
Chickpea or Chick-pea	Nutritional legume, also known as gardamzo or Bengal gram.
Chilladas	Lightly spiced lentil cakes.
Chimchurri	A Greek sauce made from garlic, parsley and oregano.
Chinese Leaves	Crunchy Chinese cabbage which can be eaten raw or cooked.
Chining	Involves cutting the rib bones from the back-bone in meat joints of beef, lamb or pork.
Chipotle paste	A paste made from ground smoked chipotle chillies which gives a spicy earthy taste to Mexican food.
Choriso	Italian sausage.
Choron sauce	Bearnaise sauce flavoured with tomato puree; used with grilled meat or fish dishes.
Chowder	A thick, stew-like, soup made from shellfish with pork or bacon.
Chump Chops	A cut of either pork or lamb taken from the lower back of the animal.
Clafoutis	A batter, the substance of which resembles a light cake mixture when cooked.
Clapshot	(From Scotland). Mashed potatoes, and swede or turnips.
Clarifying	The dividing of fat from water or other liquids, e.g. gravy.
Cobbler	A baked pudding which can be a meat dish e.g. Beef Cobbler, or a fruit dessert covered with a sponge topping. Or, more usually with meat, and a topping of little dough discs.

Cock-a-leekie	A substantial Scottish soup made from chicken stock, leeks and prunes, to which cooked beef may be added.
Coddling	A method of soft boiling eggs.
Colcannon	A traditional Irish dish, mainly consisting of mashed potatoes with kale or cabbage with butter, salt and possibly onions added. When fried together it is similar to bubble and squeak.
Coleslaw	Sliced cabbage based salad in mayonnaise
Collared	Boiled, pickled or salted meat served cold.
Collop	A small portion or slice of cooked meat, served hot or cold.
Combo Platter	(Combined Plate). A little of everything; two or more meats or surf and turf.
Compote	Fruit stewed with sugar. Can be served either hot or cold.
Conde	A dessert consisting of creamed rice combined with fruit and red jam sauce.
Conde, À la	Usually means including rice. Also, the name of a type of pâtisserie.
Confectioners' Custard	A vanilla filling for cakes and sweet pastries; made from a sweet white sauce with added egg yokes.
Confit	(Of duck or goose for example). Refers to food cooked slowly in its own fat at low temperature.
Conserves	Preserved fruit and vegetables to be used at a later date as a sweet or savoury condiment e.g. jams jellies, chutneys, pickles or relishes.
Consommé	A clear soup.
Coring	To remove pips and membranes from apples and pears etc.
Corkage	A charge made by a restaurant or hotel for serving wine brought-in by a customer.

Cornichon	Gherkins.
Coronade	(Of beef) – Essentially a beef casserole topped with French bread spread with French mustard.
Coulis	Sweet reduction sauce or a rich gravy made from concentrated meat or poultry juices.
Court Bouillon	A liquid prepared for poaching fish.
Couscous	A North African semolina dish traditionally cooked by steaming and served with meat or vegetables.
Crécy, À la	Made from or garnished with carrots.
Crème Anglaise	(English cream). A light pouring custard used as a dessert cream or sauce. A mixture of milk, sugar and egg yokes.
Crème Brulée	Burnt cream dessert.
Crème Fraîche	The French version of soured cream. It is rich and thick and made from pasteurised cows' milk to which a lactic bacteria culture is added. This thickens the cream and gives it a distinctive sharp flavour.
Crème Pâtissiere	Custard cream. An alternative to fresh cream for pastry fillings.
Cremets	Soured sweetened milk desserts which resemble thick cream, usually served with fruit
Crêpes	Pancakes.
Crevettes	French for 'prawns'.
Crimping	Either to pinch around the double crust edge of a pie or tart or to make cuts into (usually large) fish to allow heat penetration, or to trim various fruit and vegetables such as cucumber, to produce a decorative finish.
Croissant	A pastry-like bread in the shape of a crescent.

Croquembouche, Croque-en-bouche	A French dessert attractively presented as a cone of profiteroles or meringues. This dessert can be filled with fruit and cream, or fruit and cream can be served separately. See also 'Profiteroles'
Croque Monsieur	Baked ham and cheese sandwich, dipped in beaten egg before being baked or grilled.
Croquettes	A savoury, usually neatly shaped, deep fried, using minced or mashed vegetables, meat or fish.
Crudités	Raw vegetable selection served with sauces or dips as a starter.
Cruller	An American fancy shaped fried dough bun; very similar to doughnuts.
Crumpets	(Also known as Pikelets). Griddle baked cakes in metal rings. Picklets are baked without rings to hold them.
Crustaceans	Shellfish, such as lobsters, prawns,crayfish crabs and shrimps.
Cuit à point	Done to a turn.
Cuit, pas assez	Underdone.
Cuit, trop	Overdone
Cuisine	A style of cooking, characteristic of a geographical region, country or establishment.
Cullen Skink	A haddock and potato soup from Scotland.

NOTES

NOTES

D

D

Daikon	Japanese white radish or mooli radish.
Dartois	A flavoured or filled light pastry, usually served as an hors d' oeuvre.
Dauphinoise	(Of potatoes). Sliced and cooked in milk, typically with a topping of cheese.
Dolmades	(Delma or Dolmadis). Stuffed vine or cabbage leaves, usually with minced beef.
Draw, To	Removing the stomach, intestines and other internal organs, especially of birds in preparation for cooking.
Dulse	Seaweed.
Dugléré	A white flour based sauce with shallots, white wine, tomatoes and parsley. Also, a method of cooking white fish in white wine and water, adding cream and a velouté sauce.
Dunking	Is to dip a biscuit or similar into tea or coffee, to soften and release the flavour.
Dredging	To lightly sprinkle food with flour, sugar, etc.
D' agneau	Lamb.

NOTES

E

E

Echalion	'Banana' shallots.
Echinus	Edible sea urchins.
Edamame	Immature soybeans cooked in the pod and used in Chinese and Japanese cuisine
Elvers	Baby eels.
Empanada	Spanish. 'Baked in pastry'. These pastry-like turnovers can be filled with meat and vegetables or filled with fruit as a dessert.
Empanadas	Little pastry parcels containing highly flavoured savoury filling. A tapas style snack.
En broche	Roasted or grilled on a spit or skewer.
En croûte	In pastry.
Endive	A type of lettuce with very crinkly leaves. Has very short shelf life. Sold as 'frissée'.
En papillote	(Fr. 'In parchment'). Vegetables or meat baked in folded paper or foil for steaming food.
Entrée	Main course, The main event or main dinner dish.
Entrecôte (Beef)	Denotes a prime cut of beef used for steak. A traditional entrecote comes from the rib area.

Escabeche	A term for Mediterranean dishes containing either poached or fried fish or chicken, pork or rabbit which has been marinated in an acidic mixture before serving.
Escalope	A thin slice of meat.
Espagnole Sauce	A rich thick sauce with bacon, vegetables, brown sauce and tomato puree as a base.

NOTES

NOTES

F

F

Falafal	An Arabic dish consisting of deep fried patties or balls made from ground chickpeas and added spices.
Farce or Mousseline	A mixture of finely ground fish, meat or poultry, mixed with egg, cream or flavourings. Can be used as a stuffing or served alongside a main dish.
Farinata	An Italian crispy pancake made with chickpea flour, olive oil and water.
Farro	A nutty flavoured wheat grain mixture with a chewy texture.
Fenugreek	A herb which can be used in leaf or powdered form, often used in Indian cuisine.
Fermentation	Chemical breakdown by bacteria or micro-organisms such as yeast.
Fettuccine	Noodles.
Fig Sly	Consists of a shortcrust pastry covered by minced dried figs, raisins and walnuts which are then covered by a second layer of pastry, then baked. Very common in N.W. England.
Fig Sly Cakes or 'cheats'	A deceptively plain looking cake, but filled with a rich filling of figs, nuts and dried fruits.

Filo Pastry	Very thin layers of pastry made from unleavened dough.
Finger Food	Usually snacks and nibbles.
Flageotes	A variation of haricot bean.
Flan	An open tart, cooked in a ring.
Fleuron	Small fancy shaped pastry used for garnishing entrees, vegetables, etc.
Florentine	Is a pastry of French or Italian origin, made from hazel or almond nuts, candied cherries mixed with sugar, butter and honey. They often have a chocolate coated base.
Focaccia	An Italian oven baked flat bread.
Fondant	An icing or topping for cakes and fancies.
Fondue	Melted cheese dish.
Fontina	Italian cheese; excellent for cooking.
Fool, or Mousse	A creamy dessert.
Frangipane	A sweet filling incorporating almonds.
Frappé	Iced, frozen or chilled.
Freekeh	A whole grain young green wheat which has been toasted. Similar to Bulgur wheat.
Fricassée	Is a method of cooking meat in which it is cut-up, sautéed and braised in its own stock and served with a thick white sauce.
Frit	Fried.
Frittata	A type of Italian Omelette using eggs and vegetables and possibly meat and/or cheese.
Fritters	Small portions of meat, fish or vegetables, coated in batter or breadcrumbs and fried.
Friture	Fried food.
Ful Medames	Round beans of floury texture. A basic ingredient in Egyptian cooking.
Fumet	A concentrated stock, usually of game or fish, used as a flavouring.

NOTES

G

G

Galangal	Thai ginger. Has a mild peppery flavour.
Galantines	Meat or poultry stuffed and dressed, lightly fried, boiled and then glazed with jelly and decorated. Served when cold.
Ganache	A glaze, icing, sauce or filling for pastries made from chocolate and cream.
Gazpacho	Cold soup made from pureed salad ingredients, often served with a side garnish.
Gastronomy	The study and cookery associated with a particular region. The practice or art of choosing, cooking and eating good food.
Gâteau	A cake.
Gibelotte	A rabbit casserole common to Northern France, or a Canadian rabbit and tomato soup.
Gigot d'Agneau en Croûte	Leg of lamb in pastry.
Gim	See 'Nori'
Girolles	Mushrooms.
Glacé	Can mean either, iced, frozen or having a smooth, glossy surface or glaze. Can be either sweet or savoury.
Glazing	To give a glossy surface or finish to sweet or savoury food.

Gluhwein	A spiced mulled wine.
Gluten	A mixture of proteins found in wheat, barley and rye. It helps dough rise and gives a chewy texture.
Gnocchi	Italian dumplings made of semolina, wheat flour, eggs and cheese. Often eaten as a first course. Alternatively, fancy shapes of semolina paste used as a garnish for soups and other savoury dishes.
Gochugaru	Korean red chilli powder.
Gochujang	Korean red chilli paste.
Goji or Wolf Berries	An Asian fruit often consumed in dried fruit form as in cereals or fruit juices
Goujons	Small strips of chicken, fish or meat generally coated in egg and breadcrumbs
Gourmet	Connoisseur of good food
Grana Padano	An Italian hard cheese.
Gratin	Topped with or layered with cream or cheese, sprinkled with breadcrumbs and browned under a grill or in a hot oven.
Gratin Dauphinois	A baked potato dish made from layered potatoes and cream or cheese.
Gravlax, Gravadlax	Dry-cured salmon.
Gremolata, Gremolada	A chopped condiment made of zest of lemon, parsley and garlic. A traditional Italian accompaniment to braised veal shank.
Grenita	A frozen dessert made from fruit, wine and sugar.
Gribiche	Classic French sauce, similar to tartare.
Grilse	Young salmon.
Griotte	Morello cherries.
Guacamole	An avocado-based dip.
Guava	Fruit of a tropical tree.

Guinea Fowl or Pintade	Now a domestic bird, with a 'gamy' taste, somewhere between chicken and pheasant, but quite dry.
Gumbo, Okra or Ladies Fingers	Small green seed pods used as a vegetable, or in soup.
Gurnet	A form of gunard fish.
Gyoza	Oriental pan-fried dumplings

NOTES

H

H

Hache, **Hachis**	Minced or chopped.
Haggis	Scotland's national dish. A large mutton sausage using the offal of the sheep (heart, liver, lights and paunch), plus onions, oatmeal herbs and whisky.
Halloumi	A Cypriot semi hard cheese made from sheep milk.
Harissa dressing or sauce	Of North African origin, consisting of chillies, roasted peppers, herbs and vegetable or olive oil.
Haslet	Pigs' offal.
Haute Cuisine	High quality cooking, carefully prepared and usually presented in the French style.
Hindle Wake	"Hen of the Wake". Hen to be eaten during the fair.
Hogget	A sheep that is between 1 and 2 years old. It has a much more intense flavour than younger lamb, and slow cooking tenderises it and brings out the flavour.
Hollandaise Sauce	A white wine and egg based sauce.
Homing	An American cereal made from maze.
Homus bi Tahini	A chick pea and tahini based dip.
Hors d'oeuvre	Starters, small hot or cold snacks.

Huffins Traditional flat loaves with deep indentations, open texture and a soft crust, served for tea, sliced and buttered.

NOTES

NOTES

I

I

Ifta (Arabic Breakfast)	The evening meal when the fast is broken during Ramadan; Usually consists of small portions of fried vegetables often in pastry parcels.
Infusion	The process of extracting chemical compounds or flavours from plant materials in a solvent such as water, oil or alcohol, by allowing the material to remain suspended in the solvent – often called 'steeping'. An infusion is also the resultant liquid.
Ingredients	Are the components which made-up a recipe.
Irish Moss	See 'Carrageen'

NOTES

J

J

Jerk Sauce	A Jamacan Spicy sauce used in the preparation of meat or fish by marinating or dry rubbing
Jerky	American dried beef. See also under 'Biltong'.
Julep	A refreshing drink, often with a milk base, of wine or spirits. It is usually infused with mint and served with ice.
Julienne	Food cut into long thin strips like match sticks, e.g. shoestring fries, carrots julienne, celery and onions. Often used for stir-fry.
Jumbles	Simple shaped cookies or biscuits.
Junket	A milk based dessert using rennet and sugar.
Jus	Reduction of savoury liquids or natural juices.

NOTES

K

K

Kaffir	Lime leaves, small and shiny.
Kaisen gyoza	Dumplings with Salmon and shiitake mushrooms.
Kaisen ten	Soft shell crab, king prawns, white fish and squid in crispy batter with ginger and soy dipping sauce.
Kala namak	Black rock salt.
Kedgeree	A smoked haddock dish containing rice, hard-boiled eggs and peas.
Kendal Mint Cake	A glucose based mint chocolate bar, which is a popular source of energy widely used by climbers.
Kentish Huffkins	A soft yeast dough loaf with a deep indentation in the centre which can be filled with fruit.
Ketchup or Catsup	A sauce or dressing usually of tomato or mushroom.

Khorasan or Oriental Wheat	Is similar to ordinary wheat which can be milled into flour and is commonly used in breakfast cereals, pancakes and waffles.
Kikkoman	Matured soy sauce.
Kitcheree	An Indian dish made from mung beans and basmati rice.
Kohlrabi	A stem vegetable with green foliage and a turnip-like globe.
Korma, qorma	Any variety of Indian dish braised with stock, yogurt or cream.
Kotlety	Of Eastern European origin, composing ground meat, eggs, bread, onions, oil and water moulded into croquettes or patties and lightly fried in breadcrumbs, before final cooking in an oven.
Koulibiaka	A Russian speciality which is generally served hot as a starter or as an hors d' oeuvre. Can also refer to a Russian fish pie containing semolina.
Kromeski	Polish name for a sort of croquette, butter coated and deep fried.
Kumquat	A small orange or yellow sub-tropical fruit with sweet and slightly bitter flavour. Can be eaten raw or cooked and used in preserves.

NOTES

NOTES

L

L

Lactose	A type of sugar found in milk.
Ladies Fingers	See 'Okra'. – A term used for sponge fingers and Boudoir biscuits.
Laksa	Malay/Chinese cuisine: Spicy noodle soup containing either fish or chicken.
Lancashire Hot Pot	A traditional lamb stew which includes potatoes, onions and mushrooms.
Larder	A cupboard or room where food is stored.
Larding	Inserting small strips of fat bacon into the flesh of game birds or meat to prevent the flesh from drying out during cooking. See also 'Barding'.
Lardons	Small chunks of dried bacon used to give a good salty depth of flavour to savoury dishes and salads.
Lardy Cakes	A yeast dough cake containing lard and mixed fruit.
Lasagne	A pasta dish with a Bolognese sauce.
Laver	A seaweed used as a vegetable, or to make into bread. See also 'Nori'.

Lawand	A dish using mutton in a curry sauce and served with rice.
Lebkuchen	A festive German hard ginger cake decorated with almonds and sugar.
Lomper	Norwegian tortillas, made from potatoes and various flours. Can be used as wraps for sweet or savoury fillings.
Lovage	A herb.
Luting	A strip of pastry used to seal a pastry lid or cover.

NOTES

NOTES

M

M

Maesil	Korean plum extract.
Macaroni	A tubular pasta. e.g. Penne.
Macaroon.	Small circular cakes, primarily made from almonds and/or coconut, mixed with sugar, egg-whites and other flavourings.
Magluba	Means 'up-side-down'.
Maison	A dish in the style of the particular restaurant.
Maitre d' hôtel, or Maitre	(French for Master of the house). The person in charge of the dining experience.
Maitre d' hôtel butter	A butter moulded together with lemon juice, parsley, salt and pepper and chilled.
Maitre d' hôtel dressing	A dressing for steaks, mixed grills and fish.
Maldon	A salt.
Malt	An extraction from cereal grain using soaking followed by hot air drying.
Manchego	A Spanish cheese.
Mange tout	French for 'Eat all'. Very young peas in their pods. See also 'Sugar Peas'.

Marinade	The technique of tenderising, and adding extra flavour to food, usually meat, by soaking it in a mixture of oil, vinegar and seasoning before cooking.
Marmite	(Fr. 'little pot'). A yeast extract spread, containing vegetable concentrates and vitamins.
Matcha	The finely ground green leaves of the Japanese tea plant.
Matzos, Matzoth, Motzah, Matzo or Matza	Jewish unleavened brittle bread or biscuit, eaten during Passover.
Mealie	South African name for maize
Medlars	The fruit rather like a small brown apple with a rose hip appearance. The flesh when 'bletted' or overripened is brown and soft and can be eaten raw. When unbletted the flesh is white. Medlars make excellent jams, jellies and cheeses.
Medley	A mixture of, as in vegetables, or a selection of various food groups.
Medallions	A circular helping of food, particularly from a boneless cut of meat. An individual quantity of food taken as part of a meal.
Mendiannts	French celebratory chocolate disks decorated with dried fruit and nuts representing monastic colours and orders.
Menu	Bill of fare.
Meunière, (à la meunière)	To cook by dredging in flour, especially fillets of fish. A meuniere sauce is a simple preparation of brown butter, chopped parsley and lemon juice.
Meza (Arabic for table)	Small plates of dips and salads, intended to be shared around the table. Frequently an appetizer for a meal. Commonly found in the Middle East.
Mignon	Means small and dainty, as in fillets of beef.

Millefeuilles	Classic French pastries made from many thin layers of puff pastry, usually filled with cream and jam.
Montmorency (as in à la Montmorency)	Name given to various sweet dishes and cakes which include cherries
Mirepoix	A mixture of onions, celery, carrots and perhaps pieces of bacon finely chopped and sautéed in fat and used as a base on which to braise meat.
Mirin	A Japanese mild, sweet rice cooking wine.
Mirliton, Mirleton	See 'Chayote'.
Mirlitons	Little Genoese cakes sitting on a macaroon bed, in a pastry case.
Miroton	A French beef stew in an onion flavoured sauce.
Miso Paste	A traditional Japanese seasoning made by fermenting soya beans with salt and a fungus called Koji. A basic flavouring in most Japanese cooking.
Mizuna	A peppery flavoured Japanese salad green of the Brassica family.
Molluscs	Rock clinging shell fish e.g. Mussels, oysters, scallops, cockles and whelks.
Morcilla	Spanish black pudding.
Mornay Sauce	A reduced Béchamel sauce with cheese and butter incorporated.
Mortadella	An Italian sausage made from ground heat-cured pork and flavoured with spices.
Morue	Salt cod.
Mooli or Daikon	Mild flavoured radishes.
Mouli	A hand operated utensil designed to push food through a grating disc to give a very fine texture. Ideal for making a puree or baby-food.

Moussaka	A Greek dish made from minced beef or lamb, aubergines and other vegetables and topped with a cheese sauce.
Mousse	A sweet or savoury light mixture which can be served either hot or cold. See also 'soufflés'.
Mousseline	See 'Farce' and 'Hollandaise Sauce'.
Muesli	A breakfast cereal mix of grains, flakes, seeds and fruit.
Mulligatawny Soup	A curry flavoured soup which includes eggs and tomatoes.
Muffins	See 'Pikelets'.

NOTES

NOTES

N

N

Naan bread	Unleavened bread. Traditionally baked on the side of a tandori oven.
Navarine (of Lamb)	A dish of Mutton, potatoes and onions or mixed spring vegetables. See also 'Ragoût'.
Nasi Goreng	Indonesian dish of rice and meat (often pork), left-overs, served with a topping of egg.
Neeps	Scottish word for turnips.
Niçoise, as in Niçoise Salad	Chopped traditional salad ingredients with added anchovies, tuna, egg, new potatoes, beans, and olives.
Nigella Seeds	A spice used as a substitute for black cumin.
Noisette	A small portion of lean meat such as lamb or pork. Also a chocolate made with hazelnuts.
Nori, Gim	Japanese edible seaweed, a popular addition to Japanese meals.

NOTES

O

O

Offal	The bits that 'fell-off' the carcass e.g. heart, liver and kidneys. The edible internal bits of an animal. See also 'Haggis'.
Okra	See 'Gumbo, Ladies Fingers', above.
Omelette Arnold Bennett	A dish from the Savoy Grill, dedicated to the novelist Arnold Bennett. The omelette combines Finnan Haddock and Parmesan cheese.
Onglet or Hanger	A highly flavoured steak taken from the lower belly of a steer or heifer.
Orecchiette	A type of pasta used in southern Italy. It literally means 'Small ears'.
Organic	A food produced by organic farming.
Orzo, Risoni	A pasta which looks like large grains of rice.
Ossobucco	An Italian speciality of shin of veal braised with vegetables, white wine and stock. Frequently garnished with 'gremolata' and served with risotto.

NOTES

P

P

Pak choi	Chinese cabbage, Chinese leaves.
Paella	A Spanish rice dish.
Pain de mie	Sandwich bread.
Pain grille	Toast.
Pain perdu	French toast, mock fritters or "Poor Knights Pudding". Also, a sweet made from left-over bread or cake and flavoured with jam, cinnamon, etc.
Palmier	A flaky or puff pastry cake, sandwiched together with jam or cream.
Panacotta	(Italian: Cooked Cream) – A dessert of thickened and moulded sweet cream. It can be flavoured with rum, vanilla or coffee essence.
Panada or Panade	A thick paste made from flour, milk or water, and butter to which fish or meat is added to make a farce. See 'Farce'. Also a binding sauce.
Pancetta	Italian cured streaky bacon, or cured ham.

Panettone	Italian Christmas cake made from a light yeast dough with fruit and peel added.
Pansotti	A stuffed pasta, similar to ravioli, but does not contain meat. Instead they contain green vegetables such as spinach and herbs. Usually covered with a walnut dressing.
Parfait	Either a rich dessert made of cream, sugar, eggs and ice-cream, or several layers of different types of ice-cream, also served in a tall glass.
Parkin	Ginger cake. Originally from the North of England.
Parlick Fell	A sheep milk cheese from Northern Lancashire.
Parmigiana	An Italian dish made with fried sliced aubergine or egg-plant layered with cheese and tomato sauce, which is then baked.
Paskha, Pasha, Pashka or Pascha	An Eastern Orthodox festive dish. A Russian creamy cheese sweet dish filled with candied fruit and nuts, and usually lavishly decorated with religious symbols.
Passata	Uncooked tomato puree.
Pasta	An Italian dish made from unleavened dough of durum wheat.
Pasta all uovo	Egg pasta.
Pasta in Brodo	Skinny, (hair-like) decorative pasta, often served in soups and puddings.
Pâté	Savoury mixture of game, liver, etc, or a pie.
Pâté Brisée	A very rich short crust pastry, often used as a base for a tart or quiche because it does not puff-up during baking.
Pâté Frolle	Pastry containing ground almonds.
Pâté Moulée	A rich short crust pastry suitable for French raised pies.

Pâtisserie	A French or Belgian bakery which specialises in sweet pastries.
Paupiettes	Thin slices of lean beef rolled around a stuffing of vegetables, pork or sausage meat.
Payson	A garnish of thin rounds of onion, carrots and turnip or swede.
Peanut	Groundnut or Monkey nut. The flowers and pods are formed underground – hence the name.
Pease Pudding	A vegetable dish made from dried split peas. Can be served hot or cold.
Pecorino	Sheep cheese
Pectin	A substance used as a gelling agent and used as a stabiliser in various fruit drinks, which is mainly extracted from citrus fruit
Pemican	Dried, powdered buffalo or deer meat, prepared and used as a concentrated food.
Peperoncino, Pepperoncini	Hot chilli peppers of the capsicum family.
Perch	A fresh water game fish.
Perdreaux	Partridges less than a year old.
Perigueux Sauce	A rich Madeira flavoured brown sauce from the Perigord region of France.
Persimmon, Persimon	Formerly known as Divine fruit. They vary in size, shape and colour according to variety. Orange/yellow pulp is sweet and often used as flavouring.
Pesto	A paste composed of five ingredients; crushed pine nuts, basil, olive oil, garlic and parmesan cheese.
Phalsa Berries	An exotic subtropical fruit with a sweet tangy flavour.
Piccalilly	A vegetable preserve which needs only a short cooking time.

Pikelets	See 'Crumpets'.
Pilaff or Pilau	A richly flavoured rice dish containing small pieces of chicken or meat and many spices.
Pintade	See 'Guinea Fowl'.
Piparade	A famous egg dish from the Basque region of France. A type of omelette.
Piroshky	Russian for 'little pies'. Usually made of choux pastry shells stuffed with meat and vegetables, but other fillings can be used.
Pissaladiera	A variation of Italian pizza containing black olives.
Pistou	A cooking sause which includes garlic, olive oil and basil.
Pit	To remove stones or seeds from fruit such as olives and cherries.
Pithivier	A French Pastry. A closed puff-pastry pie with either a sweet or savoury filling.
Pizzaladière or Pissaladière	French small pizza, but made from layers of pastry, with crusty exteriors. Can be sweet, spicy, savoury and buttery.
Plantain	Look similar to bananas in colour and shape, but are longer and thicker. When cooked are treated more like a vegetable.
Plat de jour	The main dish of the day in a restaurant.
Poaching	To simmer food such as fish, very gently in milk or water or other liquids.
Poêle	A stove. (Oeuf à la poêle = Fried egg).
Polenta	A very fine golden corn meal from Italy. It can be eaten as a porridge, or cooled and solidified as a loaf, which is then baked grilled or fried. Used to make Gnocchi.
Pollock	Rock Salmon. Also known as Coley or Coal Fish. Used like Cod.

Polony also known as Bologna sausage, Balony or Lyoner	A sausage made from minced bacon, pork and veal.
Pomegranate molasses	A thick dark syrup, sweet and sharp, a versatile condiment similar to Balsamic vinegar. It can be used as a salad dressing or marinade.
Pomelo	A type of grapefruit, but larger with a thick pithy skin.
Pommes Dauphinoise	See 'Dauphinoise'.
Porcini	Italian mushrooms.
Pork Scratchings, Pork rind or Pork Crackling	Oven dried, slowly cooked pig skin.
Porterhouse (steak)	Both the T-bone and Porterhouse steaks have T shaped bones in beef steaks, with meat on both sides. The Porterhouse is cut from the rear of the sirloin so as to include more tenderloin on one side of the bone, whereas the T-bone is cut from the front end, with less tenderloin.
Portobello Mushrooms	Very large mature dark brown mushrooms
Potatoes Anna	A French dish of sliced and layered potatoes cooked in melted butter and baked until they form a cake. Can be served hot or cold with meat.
Pot au feu	Traditional French dish of meat and vegetables.
Potage Andalouse	Pumpkin soup.
Pottage	Thick meat or vegetable soup.
Poussins	Small immature birds, sometimes called 'Spring chickens'.
Praline	An almond preparation which can be used as a paste or flavouring added to creams or butter creams etc. for fillings. Also, cooled burnt sugar.

Preserves	Various methods of keeping fruit and vegetables in an edible and attractive state, which prevents decomposition, and which can be used for savoury or sweet dishes all the year round.
Prickly Pear	The watery fruit of various types of cactus, often used to make soup, salads, desserts or beverages. Also called 'Indian fig'.
Primeurs	Early forced vegetables and fruit.
Profiteroles	French choux pastry balls filled with whipped cream, custard, pastry cream, or ice-cream.
Ptarmigan	A small wild bird of the grouse family.
Pulses (grain legume)	Leguminous crop producing seeds within a pod. Used as food for both humans and animals.
Pumpernickle	German black bread.
Punchnep	A potato and swede or turnip dish.
Puris	An Indian snack of crispy pastry enclosing a spicy vegetable filling. Can also be made with minced lamb.
Purslane	A leafy vegetable with a slightly sour and salty taste which is used widely throughout Europe and the Middle East in salads, stir fries etc.
Puy Lentils	Small grey lentils which when cooked retain their shape and texture.

NOTES

NOTES

Q

Q

Qorma	See 'Korma'.
Quail	Small game birds which should not be hung, but eaten as fresh as possible.
Quark	An unsalted curd cheese, similar to cottage cheese.
Queenies	Scallops, an Isle of Man speciality. See also 'Tanrogans'.
Quenelles	Very fine smooth textured rissoles made from chicken, veal or fish, minced and mixed with butter, egg and seasoning.
Quesidilla	A Spanish wrap.
Quince	An edible fruit closely related to the apple and pear family. It is hard and quite acid and is often cooked with apples and pears and is excellent when preserved.
Quinoa	An alternative to pasta and bread.
Quorn	A meat substitute, which can be eaten by vegetarians.

NOTES

R

R

Radicchio

A leaf vegetable sometimes known as Italian chicory. It has a bitter taste which mellows on being grilled or roasted.

Ragoût or Ragoos

A thick stew of beef or other meat, poultry, game or vegetables, thickened with rich stock or sauce. See also 'Navarin'.

Ragù

Either a slowly cooked duck, or a savoury sauce produced in northern Italy, made from minced veal, streaky bacon, onions, tomatoes, herbs and oatmeal, as an all purpose sauce.

Rainbow Carrots

Modern and colourful developments of the traditional orange carrot.

Raita

A cooling side-dish for curries with a cucumber and yoghurt base.

Ramekins

Either small dishes for serving individual portions of food, or a small amount of food served separately.

Ratafia cakes

Small flat almond biscuits.

Ratatouille

A traditional Mediterranean baked vegetable dish which can be eaten hot or cold.

Réchauffés

The use of cold cooked meat prepared in various ways by heating through, but not actually getting to boiling point. See 'Miroton'.

Relish	A condiment, sauce or pickles eaten with any variety of savoury food to add interest, flavour and often colour.
Remoulade	A dressing served with fish or meat.
Remove, Relevé	The term used for the roast joint course in a formal meal. Now mostly out of date.
Rendering	To extract fat from meat trimmings through cooking.
Rennet	Preparation made from the stomach of a calf, used in cheese making and desserts e.g. junket.
Requeson	A Mexican Whey cheese.
Riboflavin	One of the B vitamins.
Rice Paper	A thin edible paper made from a plant grown in China. Used as baking sheet for delicate confectionary. It need not be removed before consuming.
Ricotta	An Italian white creamy cheese, made from whey milk.
Rigatoni	One of a group of macaroni or tubular pastas.
Rilletes	French pork pâté.
Risoni	See 'Orzo'.
Risotto	A flavoured rice dish cooked with stock and wine.
Rissols	Meat balls. Usually the mixture made cold from meat finely chopped, with flavouring and herbs, which are then bound together with an egg. After shaping, they are dipped into egg, rolled in breadcrumbs and fried.
Roesti or roschti	A Swiss dish consisting mostly of fried potatoes. It was originally a breakfast dish.
Rollmop	Uncooked pickled herring fillets.
Rose or Rock Salmon	See 'Pollock'.
Rosti	Swiss Fried Potatoes

Rot, Roti	Roast or baked poultry or game course in formal dinner menu.
Rotisserie	Either a rotating spit for roasting and barbecuing meat, or a restaurant specialising in that type of meat.
Roughage	Carbohydrates.
Roux	The mixture of fat and plain flour which forms the basis of most sauces.
Rye	A strong flavoured flour.

NOTES

S

S

Sabayon

A sweet, frothy sauce to serve with rich fruit and sponge puddings.

Saccharin

A sugar substitute.

Sacristans

Puff pastry fingers with added almonds and icing sugar; excellent accompaniment to fruit compote.

Sago.

A starch extracted from various tropical palm stems, which forms the basis of a milk pudding. Similar to rice or tapioca.

Saignant

Underdone, almost raw.

Sake

A Japanese fermented rice wine.

Salad Niçoise

See under N.

Salamagundy, salamon-gundy, salamagundi

An elaborate salad of finely minced or chopped meat, fruit, vegetables, nuts, flowers and/or eggs. Thought to relate to the French word 'salmagondis' meaning a mix of different things.

Sallet

A name given to all plants grown for eating.

Sally Lunn

A light yeast cake or bun.

Salmis

The use of pre-cooked, left-over meat e.g. chicken, reheated and served in a sauce or in pancakes or vol-au-vent cases. See also under 'Miroton' and 'Réchauffés'.

Salpicon	A forcemeat in a sauce used as a stuffing or filling.
Salsa	A sauce.
Salsa Verde	Italian green sauce.
Salsify	A white skinned parsnip-like vegetable.
Saltimbocca	Veal escalopes wrapped in parma ham.
Samphire	A coastal plant which can be pickled, eaten as a vegetable, or used in salads.
Sansho	A pepper spice.
Saracen Corn	See Buckwheat.
Sashimi	A Japanese delicacy consisting of thinly sliced raw fish or meat, often served with rice and vegetables.
Satay	An Indonesian or Malaysian grilled meat dish.
Satay Sauce	A sauce combining ground peanuts shrimp and chillis, used as an accompaniment to grilled or barbequed kebabs
Sauce Gribiche	A French mayonnaise style egg sauce, similar to tartare.
Sauce Ravigote	A sauce with French dressing base, added mixed herbs and shallots or onions.
Sauce Velouté	A white sauce made from chicken stock and white wine.
Sauerbraten	A German pot roast.
Sauerkraut	A form of fermented cabbage. Particularly good with Frankfurter sausages and pork.
Sauté	To cook lightly in fat i.e. vegetables before adding to soups and stews, in order to add flavour and to retain colour. Also potatoes cooked similarly until lightly browned.
Sea-Kale	A cabbage related vegetable found above high tide mark in England on shingle beaches.
Searing	To brown meat or vegetables quickly to lock-in juices and colour.

Secrzonera	Black rooted winter vegetables
Setting Agents	The most common are from animal origin e.g. gelatine. Usually sold in powder sachets, but vegetarian substitutes are available.
Schnitzel	Veal floured and dipped into egg and breadcrumbs, and fried or baked in oil.
Scoring	To make shallow cuts into meat or fish to help improve its flavour and help it cook more efficiently.
Shad	A European white fish.
Shawarma	Grilled meat, or meats, cooked on a turning spit for long slow cooking.
Shirring	To bake food, usually eggs, in a small shallow container.
Shitaki	Asian mushrooms, but now cultivated in Europe and the USA.
Simnel Cake	Traditional Easter Cake. Made with a layer of marzipan through the middle and topped with a marzipan cover decorated with 11 marzipan balls all around.
Singing Hinnies	Flat griddle cakes or scones. Known as fatty cakes in Scotland.
Skuets (of pork)	An early form of barbeque cooking and kebabs. A variety of tender meat and vegetables are threaded onto skewers and cooked over a grid in a shallow pan or spit grilled.
Smelt	Small fish of the salmon family. Good for frying or baking.
Snipe	A very small game bird, which requires quick light cooking and should not be drawn.
Sommelier	A specialist trained in wine and food preparation. In fine dining circles he is considered to be on a par with the executive chef.

Sorbitol	A sugar substitute.
Soubise	A purée or sauce of rice and onions, or of onions alone. Similar to Béchamel sauce.
Soufflé	A baked egg dish which is combined with either savoury or sweet ingredients, depending on whether it is to be served as a main dish or a dessert.
Souse	To cover food, often fish, with a mixture of vinegar, water and spices, and then usually cooked in the mixture.
Souvakia	Greek kebabs.
Soy, or Soya Sauce	Made from fermented soy beans and wheat. Heavily used in all varieties of Chinese cooking.
Soya	The most highly nutritious of all beans. Due to their bitter flavour they are best consumed in flour form.
Spaghetti	A pasta produced in the form of long solid strings.
Spaghetti Carbonara	A classic Italian spaghetti dish made with egg sauce, crème fresh, Italian sheep's cheese and pancetta.
Spam	Tinned precooked shoulder of pork and ham
Spanish Omelette	An omelette made with added potato.
Spatchcocked or Spattle-cocked	A cooking technique applied to game birds or young poultry where the backbone, and often the sternum have been removed before grilling or roasting. When the bird is flattened, this is known as' butterflying'.
Sprats	An oily cheap fish. Larger varieties are best grilled. Smaller sprats are sold as 'brislings' and can be served as hors d'ouvre, or as a snack on toast.

Spun Sugar	Sugar and glucose heated to the right degree to form a substance which can be 'spun' into fine sugar threads, by using forks or a sugar spinner.
Squab	A young pigeon: good in pies.
Squash	Gourd-like fruit. Some types are edible, whilst others are suitable only for decorative purposes.
Sriracha	A hot chilli sauce.
Star Anise	One of the main spices in Chinese food with a strong aniseed flavour.
Stargazy Pie	A Cornish dish made from baked pilchards together with eggs and potatoes covered with a pastry crust.
Starters	Small hot or cold snacks.
Steak Diane	An American pan fried beefsteak served with a sauce.
Stracciatella	Roman egg drop soup, or an ice-cream with strands of chocolate added.
Strudle	An Austrian layered pastry usually served with a sweet filling.
Succotash	An American dish comprising a mixture of sweet corn and beans, flavoured with chillies, basil, mint and garlic Other vegetables may be added.
Sucrose	A common sugar; obtained from both sugar beet and sugar cane.
Suet	The fat surrounding the kidneys and loin of sheep and bullocks.
Sugar Peas	See 'Mange tout'.
Sukiyaki	A Japanese dish of a kind of stew cooked at the table.
Sumac	A spice used in Levantine, Turkish and Arabic cuisine. Also used as a beverage known as 'Indian lemonade' in North America.

Sundae	An ice-cream dessert.
Supreme	The best or most delicate part, e.g. the breast of chicken.
Sushi	Japanese rice dish which includes uncooked seafood, vegetables, and sometimes tropical fruit.
Syllabubs	A drink or dish made of milk or cream, curdled by adding cider or wine and subsequently sweetened and flavoured.

NOTES

NOTES

T

T

Tabasco	A very hot red sauce of Mexican origin.
Tabbouleh, or Tabouleh	An Arabian dish made from Bulgur wheat cooked and mixed with finely chopped herbs. Served cold as a salad.
Table d' Hôte	A fixed meal consisting of a number of courses at a fixed price. There is usually a choice of dishes within each course.
Tagliata	A dish of seared steak cut into slices and served with rocket and Parmesan cheese
Tagliatare	Italian for 'tailored', or 'to cut'.
Tagliatelle, Tagliolini	A type of flat spaghetti. A variety of pasta enriched with egg and sometimes with spinach.
Tahini	An oily paste made from ground sesame and chick pea seeds – used in Eastern Mediterranean cuisine. Available in Health food shops and specialist food shops. See 'Hummus'.
Taleggio	A mild soft Italian cheese.
Tamari	Wheat free Soy sauce.
Tangelo or Ugli fruit	A hybred citrus fruit. A cross between a tangerine and a grapefruit.
Tanrogans	Scallops. Minature scallops are called 'queenies'.
Tapas	See 'Empanadas'.

Tapenade	An olive, caper and anchovy paste used generally as a versatile dip.
Tapioca	A cereal obtained from roots of the cassava plant. Usually sold as 'pearls' or flakes.
Taramasalata	A creamy dip or spread made from smoked cod roes.
Tartare	A finely minced or diced raw meat or fish dish.
Tartare Sauce	A mayonnaise or aioli based sauce of coarse texture
Teff	Gluten free flour made from the seeds of Ethiopian Wheat – similar to Quinoa. Both are used in a similar manner to wheat flour.
Tempura	Japanese small bites of batter coated vegetables and prawns, deep fat-fried and served with a dipping sauce.
Tenderstem	A cross between Chinese Kale and Broccoli. As the name implies the stem and flower can be eaten.
Terrine	An earthenware cooking dish which gives its name to the potted meat, game, foul or fish cooked in it.
Teriyaki	A rather sweet Japanese sauce often served with steak in the same dish.
Textured Vegetable Protein (TVP), or Textured Soya Protein (TSP)	A protein resembling meat.
Thiamine	One of the B series of vitamins.
Tiramisu	A rich creamy Italian dessert made from cream cheese, cream. sponge fingers, coffee and flavouring, but no fruit.
Tofu	Made by pressing the curds of coagulated soy milk into blocks which are used in S.E. Asian cuisine.

Tomato passata	A thick Italian sauce.
Tonka	Tonka beans are black and wrinkled with a smooth centre. They are used as a vanilla substitute, particularly in French cuisine.
Torte	A rich cake made with crumbs and eggs. Also contains fruit and nuts.
Tortellini	Filled tubular shapes of pasta.
Tortilla	Spanish potato omelette.
Tournedos	Slices of steak cut from the fillet and tied around with string to resemble a prepared round of beef. Also known as a 'noix' in France. These are topped with a small piece of fat and served on croutons of bread or buttered toast.
Trahanas	A traditional Greek dried food, being a mixture of bulgur wheat and milk, or of milk and yogurt, which when made into a thick soup form with tomato paste and feta, can be used to stuff vegetables, in place of rice.
Tripe	The edible lining of the stomach of cattle. See 'Offal'.
Truffles	A type of fungus, black or white and highly prized as a luxury food. They are sweet and syrupy in flavour and often used as flavouring for desserts or pasta.
Truites aux Armandes	Trout with almonds.
Truss	To prepare poultry or game for roasting by tying and skewering the legs and wings
Tuile	A baked wafer, frequently arched shaped made from dough and served as an accompaniment to other dishes.
Tureen	A deep covered dish from which soups and stews are served.
Turmeric	A distinctive yellow spice used in curry. Also gives mustard its bright yellow colour.

Txakoli or Chacoli	A very dry Spanish white wine, similar to vinegar.
Tzatziki	A Middle Eastern salad comprising yogurt, cucumber, mint and garlic. Sometimes olive oil and red wine is included in the mix.

NOTES

NOTES

U

U

Ugli fruit	See 'Tangelo'.
Umami	A basic flavour used in Japanese cooking combining sweet, sour and savoury sensations.
Unleavened Bread	Flat breads made without raising agents. e.g. Matzos.
Usquebaugh	Celtic form of the word 'Whisky', meaning 'water of life'. Also an Irish liqueur made from spiced brandy or whisky.
Udon Noodles	Japanese wheat flour noodles.

NOTES

V

V

Veal	The meat of young calves. It is very lean, tender meat with virtually no fat or membrane.
Veal Cordon Bleu	Veal as a schnitzel but topped with a slice of ham and mozzarella cheese; often heated until the cheese melts.
Veal Romagnola	Veal prepared as for schnitzel, but layered with chopped salted tomatoes between ham and mozzarella cheese, oven heated until the cheese melts.
Velouté	A white sauce made from chicken stock and white wine.
Verjuice	(Green Juice). A highly acidic sour juice, usually made from pressed crab apples or unripe grapes, or other sour juices. Spices and/ or herbs may be added. Used as a condiment, or an ingredient in salad dressing.
Vermicelli	A pasta, similar to spaghetti.
Vichy, à la.	Indicates prepared with, or garnished with, carrots.
Victuals.	Food or provisions.
Vienna Steak	Cakes of minced beef flavoured with onions, herbs and sauce, then cooked in a covered frying-pan.

Vinaigrette, à la	A dressing of oil, vinegar and herbs.
Vol-au-vent	A light rich puff pastry case filled with any finely minced meat, game, poultry, fish etc. in a suitable sauce, and served as an entrée, main or buffet meal.

NOTES

NOTES

W

W

Wasabi	Japanese horseradish.
Wheat	A grain grown in most parts of the world which provides flour for human consumption.
Whelks	See 'Molluscs'.
Whey	The watery liquid which separates from the curd when milk is clotted.
Whim-wham	A trifle (of Scottish origin) with high alcohol content.
Wholemeal Flour	Contains the whole grain, including the bran.
Wiener Schnitzel	Escalope of veal, Viennese style.
Woodcock	Considered to be the most desirable of all game birds. It is usually 'hung' for about 3 days. Woodcock is not 'drawn' before cooking except for the gizzard, which must be removed. It is best roasted.

NOTES

X, Y, Z

Y

Yakitori	Skewered, grilled chicken marinated in either sweet or sweet-sour sauce.
Yam	Resembles a sweet potato.
Yeast	A living organism used as a raising agent in bread making.
Yogurt	A bacterial fermentation of milk.
Yuzu	Japanese citrus fruit resembling grapefruit, with an aromatic flavour.

NOTES

Z

Za'atar	A condiment made from herbs and sesame seeds used in Middle Eastern cuisine.
Zabaione	An Italian sweet meaning 'egg punch'. It can be made in different ways for a hot or cold serving.
Zabaglione	A sweet Italian dessert, sauce or drink similar to Sabayon, but thicker. See 'Sabayon'.
Zest	The thin oily outer skin of citrus fruit; used grated or thinly shredded.
Zucchini	Courgettes, marrows or squash.

NOTES

Bibliography

Title	Author/Publisher
Around the World Series	IMP Ltd.
Amy Willcock's Aga Seasons.	Ted Smart/The Book People Ltd.
Creative with Cream.	Lorna Walker Octopus Books.
Dairy Book of Family Cooking.	The Milk Marketing Board.
Delia Smith's Cookery Course. Part 1	BBC Books.
Delia's Classic Edition.	BBC Books.
Delia's Winter Collection.	BBC Books.
Farmhouse Cookery – Country Kitchen.	Reader's Digest Ass. Ltd.
Favourite Game Recipies.	J. Salmon Ltd.
Four Seasons with Potatoes	Potato Marketing Board.
Good Housekeeping – Cookery Encyclopedia.	Good Housekeeping Institute.
Hamlyn All Colour Cook Book.	Hamlyn.

Home Preparation of Fruit and Vegetables.	Min. of Agric. Fisheries and Food. HMSO.
Neff Entertaining	Good Housekeeping.
Safeway Recipe Book.	Nina Froud/Safeway/Elm Tree Books.
Slow Cooker Recipe Book.	Catherine Atkinson/Southwater.
Tagines.	Lakeland/Octopus Publishing Group.
The Aga Book	Mary Berry/Aga Rayburn.
The Captain's Table	J. Salmon Ltd.
The Constance Spry Cookery Book	Pan Books.
The Cookery of England.	Elizabeth Ayrton/Penguin Books.
The Dairy Book of British Food.	Milk Marketing Board.
The New Art of Cooking.	Stork Cookery Service.
The New Complete Book of Cookery.	Summit Books/ Hamlyn Pty.
The Victorian Kitchen.	Jennifer Davies / BBC Books.
National and Local Newspapers and Magazines	Many and various.
Menus	Many and various.

www.ingramcontent.com/pod-product-compliance
Lightning Source LLC
Chambersburg PA
CBHW031628040426
42452CB00007B/732